Rose Arbor

First published by Dog Ear Publishing
4010 W. 86th Street, Ste H
Indianapolis, IN 46268
www.dogearpublishing.net

dog **ear**
PUBLISHING

ISBN: 978-159858-529-2

This book is printed on acid-free paper.

Printed in the United States of America

Dedication

I lovingly dedicate this book to
my beloved husband, Carl Arolin, for his love and
encouragement during our many years of marriage,
and for understanding my dedication to the writing
of my poetry and short stories.

Acknowledgements

To my children, Kathi, Shari, Renee, Sandy and Teddy,
for their inspiration and moral support.

And, to my wonderful friend and fellow poet, Ellen Moser,
for helping to bring this book to fruition.

Cover Illustration

To my grandson, Jeremy Newman, for sketching a
magical illustration of a rose arbor
for the cover of this book of poetry.

Table of Contents

◈

കൈ

꧁

❧

The Rose

Nature's pearly dewdrops
Are wine to the budding rose.
Just a sweet, gentle kiss
Can magically transpose,
A barren thorn-filled branch
To beauty personified.
Just one sip and the budding rose
Swells with pride.

cᴐᴑᴑᴑ

Lovely Transformation

The stream is running free now
She's finally been released.
The ice that held her bondage
Has, at last, appeased.

The infant, spring, emerges
Soft and fresh and new.
And wears her blossomed bonnets
Of pastel pink and blue.

What a lovely transformation
Has taken place once more.
For glorious springtime
Is waiting at my door.

ↄﻮ໑ৄ

Togetherness

It's been a lovely afternoon,
We've seen the sights of town.
We've helped to roll the sidewalks up,
And pull night's curtain down.

It's been a lovely, lovely day.
And, we've walked hand in hand.
From morning until eventide,
And oh, it's been so grand.

Rummage Sale

I used to save
The silliest things.
Old rubber bands
And butterfly wings.

My tastes are more
Refined today.
There's nothing
I will throw away.

My attic's packed
And overflows.
My treasure trove
Just grows and grows.

I sort them out,
But to no avail.
It's time for another
Rummage sale.

✆✇✈

No Place Like Home

I've traveled across the ocean
To Rome and gay Paree!
I've seen majestic mountains
The Mediterranean Sea.
I've seen the western prairie
Where the mighty buffalo roam.
But, in all these travels,
It'll be good to be home.

I've seen bright cactus blooming
Stood at the canyons edge.
I've viewed plaques and monuments
Teetered on the mountain's ledge.
I've enjoyed the grandeur of
Opera houses and cathedral domes,
And yet, there doesn't seem to be,
Anyplace like home!

 birds

Dieter's Lament

I'm forever counting calories,
Passing up the good stuff.
I say silly things like
"No thanks, I've had enough".

It's a battle, all uphill.
I struggle for success.
I use, for inspiration,
A stunning size ten dress,

I measure out each morsel.
Read labels religiously.
I graze on fresh green veggies
And, gallons of herbal tea.

My stomach growls and grumbles.
I've grown listless and pale.
Sure enough, I'm up five pounds
When I step on the scale.

಼ఠ಍ఠ಍

How Do I Describe A Sunset

How do I describe a sunset?
No two are quite the same.
One night the suns a golden coin,
The next, a burning flame.

Sometimes the skies are lavender
And tinged with sapphire blue.
Sometimes with shades of apricot
With gray and fuchsia too.

I can't describe a sunset,
To give it its due.
So, I'll sit back to enjoy
Each breathtaking view.

Autumn's Masterpiece

A palate rich in red and umber.
Golden coins too great to number.
Mounds of leaves in russet hues
Beneath a patch of satin blue.

I fall humbly to my knees
In praise of autumn's masterpiece.
A vibrant palate to enthrall
In GOD'S open air cathedral.

❦

Solitude

Lovely trees surround me
In peaceful solitude,
Breezes whisper softly
And set the evening mood.

Half the moon is hiding,
It's playing peek-a-boo,
In a sky of dusky-gray
With hints of baby blue.

A lone star is twinkling,
Begging to be wished upon,
And I could lie here forever
In this cool green lawn.

I hear the crickets calling.
I wait for fireflies,
In a night so enchanting,
I dare not blink an eye.

cℓℊℴℊℴℴ

Old Love Letters

Slowly, one by one,
I burned the letters that you wrote.
Tearfully I watched
The flames devour every note.

I read each precious word
This one last time.
Now, how do I convince,
This aching heart of mine?

That you no longer love me,
That you no longer care,
That all the dreams we planned,
We will never share.

Yes, I burned those old love letters.
And I felt the teardrops start.
But, tears cannot destroy memories of you,
That live on in my heart.

❦

Autumn's World And Mine

The burnished corridor's of autumn
Are carpeted in gold's and reds.
A warm, bright yellow sun
Hangs serenely overhead.

Pheasants sample kernels
From corn stalks tall and dry.
Gaggles of geese are gathering
In autumn's gray-blue sky.

Bittersweet and grapevine
On a weathered fence entwine.
I'm thankful they are a part of,
Autumn's world, and mine.

It's Raining Leaves

It's raining gold and brown leaves
Onto the shimmering pond.
I watch burnished reds and burgundies
Until the last leaf is gone.

The stream brims with these treasures
Like little boats they float on by.
Colors deep and bold beyond all measure
Reflecting in the sapphire sky.

∽◉◉◇

Gold Fish

I always wanted goldfish,
Or so, I thought I did.
It was just a fleeting notion
When I was but a kid.

I'm still fond of goldfish,
But, the kind I really like,
Are sautéed until, lightly golden,
Walleye and Northern Pike.

Empty Pockets

My pockets are empty
But my heart overflows.
That's much more important
As my heart fully knows.

What good are riches
And coins of pure gold.
If you don't have love
And real dreams to hold.

With your arms around me
And free from all care
Then I say, sincerely
I'm a millionaire.

 perpetual

Just A Cozy Place

It needn't be a palace
With imported marble floors.
I don't want carved banisters
Or, heavy stained glass doors.

I'll have no crystal chandeliers
Or curtains of antique lace.
No need for velvet draperies,
Just a cozy little place.

Where I can open windows wide
And, breathe the warm sweet breeze.
And, listen as it whispers
To the willow trees.

Give me country comforters
And gingham curtains too.
Shutters that swing in and out,
To let in skies of blue.

I'll languish on my front porch
In an old-fashioned swing.
And greet the birds and flowers
That visit me each spring.

Lady Sun

Lady Sun
Ventured out
This morning.
Dressed in her
Amber gown.

But,
She wore her
Crimson velvet
When,
The evening's shade
Came down.

⚘

My Aunt Anne

I remember vacations,
On my Aunt Anne's farm.
Just a few days
At a time.
There was adventure
In the big hayloft.
And lovely old trees
To climb.

I remember jars of peaches
She'd canned.
Those perfectly-spiced
Golden spheres.
With fresh-baked bread,
What a memorable treat.
For a girl
In her tender years.

I remember the hugs
She gave generously
And how special
She told me I am.
Is it any wonder,
That deep in my heart,
I treasure the memory
Of my Aunt Anne?

⊱⊙⊰

Mama's Aprons

Mama's aprons, such friendly things.
She wears them, to protect her clothes.
They're fancied up with gingham strings,
And Papa's still tied, to those!

Mama sings while she's baking
Wonderful goodies to win first prize.
Her aprons are special things,
No matter what their size.

I love those big deep pockets,
Where she hides treats for me.
Mama's special aprons,
Still stir my memories.

cಿಾೲ

Yesterday's Roses

When faded petals of the rose,
Have lost their sweet perfume,
The sentiment attached to those
Still lingers on each bloom.

Then like raindrops, petals will fall,
And soon be swept away.
But, in my heart, I will recall
Roses of yesterday.

Country Travelers

We find magic and splendor
In the open countryside.
In waterways and lush green fields,
As on and on we ride.
In toppling barns and silos,
Fences, weathered gray.
Sometimes we spot a windmill,
As we go on our way.
And oh, the excitement,
Of seeing exotic birds.
Or, the old-fashioned charm,
Of spotting entire herds,
Of Jersey's, or Holstein's
Grazing contentedly.
In our nightly travels,
We're happy and so carefree.
Just like gypsy vagabonds,
Beneath the clouds and sky,
We cross rivers, pass woodlands,
It seems we almost fly.
But, we travel slowly,
So we won't miss a thing,
Along God's countryside,
Our hearts fairly sing.
Then, when we return home,
Its sheer delight
To imagine what new adventure
Awaits us the next night.

ϾᏯᎧᏄᎧ

Accept My Gratitude

I find it hard to say the words
That I should say to you.
All the thank you's that I owe
Are so long overdue.

It's difficult to express
What's really in my heart.
Now, here we are face to face,
What better place to start!!!!

Clown

Size twenty-two shoes and a big red nose,
And upside down smile, a frown I suppose.

One eyebrow goes up and one goes down.
It's a strange role, that of a clown.

He carries his face and all of his clothes,
In a tattered suitcase and nobody knows.

If he's happy or sad beneath his disguise.
They never do see the tears in his eyes.

And if his heart's a bit ragged and worn,
You'd never guess he'd ever been scorned.

He puts on his face and brings laughter and glee,
To cheer up the likes of you and me.

I have often wondered, when the spotlight goes down,
If the laughter vanishes, from the heart of a clown.

He packs up his face and his funny striped clothes,
His size twenty-two shoes and his big red nose.

When reality returns and the circus leaves town,
Do the tears then fall, from the eyes of a clown?

Substitute

We made so many lovely plans,
To hold the world within our hands.
Then, for the thrill of another's kiss,
You jeopardized all of this.

We dreamed sweet dreams so many times.
It was love, just yours and mine.
Then, for the thrill of another's touch,
You trashed a love that meant so much.

Grandma's Trunk

The attic in my grandma's house
Was filled with wondrous junque.
The thing of greatest interest was,
    Her big old leather trunk.

She'd lift the lid with a gentle grasp
And display, each time with pride,
    An album with a silver clasp,
    To keep her memories inside.

Her china doll in its gingham dress,
    Yellowed through the years.
She'd softly touch a golden tress,
    But could never hide the tears.

Then, her eyes grew big and bold,
A girlish smile crossed her face.
As her fingers touched the folds
    Of a hanky trimmed with lace.

Grandma's gone now,
    But her trunk's still there
In the attic beneath the beams.
And every time I climb those stairs,
    I step back into her dreams.

❧❦

Spring Bouquet

My sweetheart brought me roses,
Each with tapered stem,
As gold as amber sunsets,
Twelve lovely fragrant gems.

My little boy came running in
And taking time from play,
He too, offered sunny gems,
From Mother Nature's array.

My finest antique crystal
Holds this treasured display,
The roses and the dandelions
Make a lovely spring bouquet.

Morning Gold

The early morning glow is fresh and golden,
And I know if I but close my dreamy eyes
And listen to enchanting cries,
Of mourning doves and mockingbirds
And answer them with my heart's words,
I share with all this morning gold
And get back a thousand fold.
Then I open my eager eyes
And embrace a new sunrise.

∽◌◍◌∾

The Gift

I treasured each gift you brought
On many special days.
Luscious deep dark chocolates
And yellow rose bouquets.

This latest gift was startling,
And though I dare not fuss,
I found it most distasteful,
This plant they call Cactus.

I tried to camouflage it
Amid lush greenery.
I even tried to drown it.
What a catastrophe!

And then, one day, it happened.
It was truly awesome.
That prickly, unloved thing
Was ablaze with blossom.

Hands

I couldn't stop the hands of fate
Or slow the hands of time.
All I could do was comfort her
And clasp her hands in mine.

I couldn't erase her tears or pain.
It wasn't in God's plans.
I will treasure for all time
The touch of Mom's dear hands.

⌀

Of Lemon Drops

Ten thousand
Golden leaves sailed by,
Like lemon drops
Falling from the sky.

Mixed in with them
Were reds and brown,
Falling one by one
Onto the ground.

I feel the autumn winds
Start blowing
Before very long
It will be snowing.

But, now I want
My fill of lemon drops,
Showers of burnished leaves
That never stops.

It's a long long time
Until the spring
And I can't wait
For the treasures she'll bring.

My Puppy

My puppy sits on the step,
Drenched by the rain
Sleek and wet.
She tugs at my heart
And nudges me
With her cold nose.
Coaxing expectantly
Soon she's snuggled
Up by the fire.
I cater to
Her every desire
And I'm mopping puddles
Once more
From my clean
Kitchen floor.

Season's End

Tumble-down fences are wading knee deep,
In russet and gold painted leaves.
Tall chimney spires are tying smoke ribbons
Around empty branches of trees.

Pumpkins seem bronzed, all but forgotten,
And cornstalks look rusted and dry.
Autumn is dancing to breeze melodies
Geese are assembling in a slate-gray sky.

The scarecrow's work is now complete
If he could he'd boast of a job well done.
This radiant season has come to and end
And it's taken with it the warm autumn sun.

The Fabric Of Life

A bit of homespun cotton
Becomes a skirt or blouse.
A piece of chintz or poplin
Makes draperies for the house.

A length of creamy satin
Becomes a wedding gown.
And floral-print calico
Covers a quilt of down.

Some soft fuzzy flannel
Makes PJ's special things.
But you need real spun gold
To fashion Angel's wings.

⚬⚬⚬

September Magic

September's magic overflows
With colors bold and true.
Crimson-gold embellishments
Changes the old for new.

A fiery-gem kaleidoscope,
As it spirals to the ground,
Already rich, with burnished tones,
Adds to brilliant mounds.

The loveliness in this autumn scene,
Is a perfect work of art.
The portrait, Mother Nature paints,
Fills my September heart.

Please Hold

In my quest for information
I've been put on hold.
Your call will be answered in order
Time after time, I'm told.

I'm tired of listening to the voices
Of those automated machines.
How I long to converse
With real-life human beings.

༄

Recycling Is The Key

The moon and stars in unison
With land and sea and skies
Are part of our great universe
That gravity defies.

The lush trees and foliage
Supply our very air,
So, it's most imperative
We treat them all with care.

Recycling is the key
If we are to survive.
Time is of the essence
To keep the world alive.

We are just passing through.
The world is ours to borrow.
Let's pitch in, do our share
For the children of tomorrow.

Picture Perfect

I've been to the palace of Versailles
To view the paintings there.
I've often enjoyed a friend's Monet
Treasured and hung with care.

I've admired each Rockwell etching,
They brought Norman much fame.
Then, Gale drew her curtains to reveal
Hollyhocks in a window frame.

My Grandpa Couldn't Whistle

My grandpa couldn't whistle
And much to his chagrin
All the glory of that triumph
Went to his sister Ann.
She'd pucker up and then let loose
With clear and vibrant tones.
The clarity of the melodies
Brought him to his knees, alone.
But, why didn't he realize
It was quite another thing?
His sister Ann could whistle
But, man, could my grandpa sing!!!!!

**Twins
-E- and Me**

We've grown so alike, we two,
Like branches on one tree.
I recognize myself in you,
And you reflect a likeness in me.

Our thoughts are just the same,
Our actions identical.
Our lives revolve in just one vein,
It's quite methodical.

Could it be that you're my twin?
Then I would be yours too.
It would explain the qualities
You share with me, and I with you.

⦿

Our Hearts
(A Sequel To Twins)

Our hearts wear friendship,
Like precious jewels.
Polished, to an everlasting shine.

Cultured, fine honed,
This meshing of kindred spirits,
A togetherness that's yours and mine.

❦

Vagabond Dreamer

His clothes, a bit shabby,
He has holes in his shoes.
The hat on his head
Looks downright abused.

He whistles an old tune,
Thought he'd set for a spell,
Has a pocketful of pennies
For the wishin' well.

He sits on a park bench
With that gleam in his eye,
Just thinkin' up wishes
His pennies can buy.

When his pocket is empty
He looks quite content,
With the dreams he's purchased
For just a few cents.

We can't live on wishes
Or pie-in-the-sky.
But, that vagabond dreamer
Always seems to get by.

≈⦿⦿⦿≈

Blue Bird

A little bird
Of brightest blue
Flew in to greet the day,
In the rustling
Autumn breeze
In a grandiose display.

What a treat,
A striking picture
For my eager eyes
To see this little
Flash of blue
In bright autumn skies.

Bluebirds

Fluttering sapphires
Amazing things
The incredible beauty
Of, bluebirds wings.

Watching them gather
In colorful hue,
I'm struck by the drama
Of, patches of blue.

❦

Tapestry

Today I listened
To the songbirds
Whistling
Sweet melodies
As they danced
Among the branches
Of autumn's
Painted trees.
Today I picked
The blossoms
Summer
Left behind
And I walked
The garden paths
Where honeysuckle
Twined.
Today my happy
Heart sang
A joyful melody.
Today I relished
Burnished colors
Of nature's
Tapestry.

In God's Loving Hands

Who paints the trees, October's hue's,
When summertime is lost?
The one who etches window panes,
We know as old Jack Frost.

Who hangs December's prisms
To glisten in the sun?
Who drapes the lawn in emeralds,
When winter's storms are done?

Who scatters flowers through the hills,
And shells upon the shore?
Who turns the leaves to gold and crimson,
That pile up at my door?

I'm told that Mother Nature
Perfumes the summer breeze,
And dresses Ballerina's grand,
That dance in apple trees.

I ask these questions, of you now,
About all the wonders of this land,
My heart tells me the answers
Are in God's loving hands.

✿

My Dinner Guests

The table is set, it's a masterpiece.
The roast is nearly done.
I've spread my finest tablecloth,
Set out grandma's Haviland.
The silver and crystal glisten
The floral centerpiece is lovely.
Now all I need to make it extra special
Is the honor of your company.

None Other

Her hands are not so steady now.
Her eyes have lost their glow.
Her hair has turned to silver.
Her steps are getting slow.

Her mind often wanders,
And names escape her too.
There are times she speaks fondly,
Of the people she once knew.

It's hard to watch her decline,
To see smiles leave her face.
No other in this whole world,
Could take my Mother's place.

cᴐⓄⓄᴐ

Always—-In Memory Of Stevie

He was tall and lanky,
An inquisitive sort of kid.
There was a special quality
In the things he did.

He had a smile that dazzled.
Everyone liked him at the start.
He always held me spellbound,
With a two-fisted grip around my heart.

I watched him grow to manhood,
With a family of his own.
In a split second he was taken from us,
It's hard to believe he's gone.

I can't help but wonder,
And sometimes, I can even smile.
When I remember, that my kid brother,
Had incredible style.

Sun Catcher

We hung a sun catcher,
On a rainy day
Hoping to chase
All the clouds away.

It hung there forlorn,
There was no doubt.
But oh, how it sparkled
When the sun came out.

෴

Prisoner

A little rich girl
In a lonely world.
With dreams that are slipping away.

Must forever wait.
Behind a locked gate.
For her protection, they say.

Well, I'd rather be
Vagabond free,
Gathering daisies in spring.

Then spend all of my days
In lavish arrays,
Gathering sadness wealth brings.

It's Lucky

It's lucky that you've got me
To point out right from wrong.
To polish all your attributes
Be they weak or strong.

It's lucky too, that I am here.
Those times when you feel blue.
But, you're not half as lucky dear,
As I am to have you.

⌘

Paris

I strolled along the streets of Paris.
'Twas a rainy September day.
I drank a toast to romance,
At a small sidewalk café.

I marveled at the fashions,
In the Galleries Lafayette.
I toured the house of opera,
A tour I won't forget.

All the paintings in the Louvre
Were quite the sights to see.
And, from her place of honor,
Mona Lisa smiled at me.

The beautiful Arc de Triomphe
Emphatically caught my eye.
As did, all the wonders
Of the Palace of Versailles.

I made a silent promise
That someday I'd return.
To the cobblestone streets of Montmartre.
To the quaint Chey-Mere Catherine.

To Paris, the city of love.
The Moulin Rouge, the Champ-Elys'ees.
But, the next time I see Paris,
Will be a sunny April day.

cococo

Soft Lights and Music

Soft lights and music
Can never heal the scars,
Your unfaithful love left
For me to feel.

Time alone cannot erase
The things you did.
Nor, can tears wash out
The memory of a beloved face.

୧ଓଡ଼ଓ

Hero

He served his country
Proud and true.
He defended
The red, white, and blue.

They wheeled him home
In a shinny new chair
And he wondered,
Did they truly care?

His life is changed
As he sits alone.
In this lonely place,
This Veteran's home.

He didn't shirk his duty.
Our country is still free,
Remember, he did this
For you and me.

Don't forget him
This survivor.
Always remember
What he stands for.

He gave his all.
He kept us free.
Let's give him thanks
For his bravery.

Teardrops

Silvery teardrops
Are falling fast
Mingled with dreams
That didn't last.
The love we knew
Is drifting astray
Teardrops are washing
Those dreams away.
Tomorrow, the sun may shine
But, not for me.
Our love has become
Just a memory.

⚬⚬⚬

The Pages Of Memory

Softly, sweetly,
Come to me
Step from the pages
Of my memory.

Touch my heart
From that abyss.
On my cheek
Place a kiss.

Softly, dearly,
Stay with me.
Forever near
In my memory.

It's A Country Home

It's a country home I'm searching for,
With picket fence and gate.
With nicks and dents and crevices,
And hems, that are not straight.

With weathered wood and worn paint.
And wreaths of old grapevine.
An ivy-covered chimney,
With holly berries entwined.

Cattle grazing lazily
In meadows soft and deep.
The sweet scented spring breeze,
That lulls me off to sleep.

Its country living at its best,
When songbirds come to call.
And, gather at my kitchen window,
A banquet lures one and all.

Windows draped in gingham,
A welcome sign at my front door.
The scents of lilac and lavender,
That's the country home I'm looking for.

᪥

Sing A Song Of Autumn

Sing a song of autumn,
Of flaming maple leaves
The gold and lemon yellow
Of elms and aspen trees.

Sing a song of harvest time,
Of corn shocks rusted brown.
Of bright orange, ready, pumpkins,
Waiting on the ground.

Sing a song of autumn,
Of smoke spires reaching high.
Of wild geese formations
In a steel-blue sky.

Sing a song of autumn
Of a vivid season past.
Sing a song of renewed seasons
And dreams that always last.

Autumn Beckons

Aspen torch
And maple flame.
Autumn beckons
Once again.
Breathtaking hues
Sun splashed days.
Vibrant colors
On display.

❦

God's Gifts

In awe, I watch the birds in flight
Soaring through the sky.
I know that with this wondrous sight
There's a force greater than you or I.

I marvel at the maple trees
Like crimson flames aglow,
The willows and the elms
In a golden row.

I'm humbled by the beauty
That surrounds me day by day.
The birds, the trees, the flowers,
God's gifts, in generous array.

Join Us Here By The Fireside

Join us here by the fireside
On this cold and frosty night.

This glorious Christmas Eve
The ground is dazzling white.

Let voices blend in harmony.
Let love reign here tonight.

And let the Christmas star
Keep shinning bright.

cɹɘɢɔ

Country Lanes

I love to walk down country lanes,
In the early morning light.
When every thing is fresh and new,
And dewy from the night.

To linger 'neath an apple tree,
Its fragrance overwhelming.
I love to watch the Robins,
Go about their parenting.

I love the sunrise, nature's gold,
The meadows, emerald green.
The sky, a country hue,
The bluest I've ever seen.

I love the country in summer,
In winter and in the fall.
But, a country lane in springtime,
Is my favorite time of all.

Spring In Minnesota

People fly south in winter.
Just like the birds on wing.
But, return to Minnesota,
With the blossoming of spring.

Just ask a true Minnesotan,
I'm sure that he'll agree,
With the changing of the season,
It's the nicest place to be.

৩৩৩

Snowfall

Snow has fallen 'round our door
And buried window sills.
It's redefined the countryside,
And rounded off the hills.

Trees that once stood stark and bare.
Are weighted down with pearls.
And diamonds brightly glistening
In a jewel-encrusted world.

Christmastime

What a lovely time of year
This merry Christmas time,
The holly and the ivy
Are, beautifully entwined.
We hear sleigh melodies
From distant hills afar,
And rejoice, everyone,
Beneath the Christmas star.

Enchanting Day

Come walk with me, my friend
Savor the cool fresh air.
See how the pretty colors blend.
Look at spring so bright and fair.

See the crocus and the daffodils.
Walk beside the glistening stream.
Note the fancy leafy frills.
How sunbeams dance and gleam.

Come walk with me, my friend
Let your troubles fall away.
There is no problem we can't mend
On this enchanting day.

Spring Enchantment

What could be lovelier
Than new birds on the wing.
Or sparkling rivers flowing
Past gardens filled with spring.

What could be more charming
Than sunny daffodils.
Or, the wild sweet April rain
As it gently spills.

Onto fragrant lilac hedges,
Or the budding, rambling rose.
What could be more enchanting
Than any one of those?

A Lovely Golden Willow

A lovely golden willow
Stands by the river there.
And, in the glow of sunlight,
She washes her golden hair.

Long tendrils dip and sway
Each day in perfect unison.
Then, she hangs them out to dry,
In the afternoon sun.

With lovely blue bird ribbons,
Tied in your golden hair,
Willow, dear willow,
You are a lady fair.

The Harvest Moon

The harvest moon
Shines silver-white.
There's a hint of frost
In the autumn night.

The man in the moon
Smiles tenderly
And takes me back
To your memory.

I remember that night
It was harvest time
When you promised me
You'd forever be mine.

So many years
Slipped away too soon.
Still your memory returns
With each harvest moon.

⁓ৡ৹

Oh, Great Pumpkin

Last night you were just a Jack-O-Lantern.
You winked at goblins that stopped by.
Today you filled the house with aromas
Of spicy cookies and pumpkin pie.

Last night you wore that silly grin.
And sat upon the step to greet,
All the little Halloween visitors.
But, today you're the special treat.

Front Porches

Front porches add nostalgic charm,
Like in the good old days.
With rockers and potted plants,
And good old fashioned ways.

Swing and a creaking screened door,
Victorian gingerbread trim,
An invitation for dreamers
When the light of day grows dim.

A gathering spot to watch sunsets,
Front porches are comforting things.
These carefree, lattice-cathedrals,
Fit for paupers and for kings.

cᴑᴏⓞᴏᴜ

How Blessed I Am

The rain has stopped
And what a treat for my eyes,
The world is a rainbow
And inviting mud pies.

It's dew-kissed meadows,
A swirling cool breeze
Sweet fragrant air,
Fresh painted trees.

It's barefoot and blossoms
In a carefree world.
How blessed I am
To be a country girl.

Secret Garden

You cannot plant a secret garden
And keep it secret long.
For soon the birds will find it,
And fill it up with song.

Each flower with its brilliant head,
Each stalk with lofty plume,
Will shout "Come In, Come In,
And drink of sweet perfume."

The walkways of cobblestone
The tall and latticed gate,
When discovered will surely beckon,
Not a soul will hesitate.

And, if perchance, a bench is there
With violets growing all around,
One may rest and say a prayer
Where loveliness abounds.

You can't keep this garden secret
Sweet breezes will broadcast the word.
And , too the message will be spread
By every singing bird.

Oh, how wonderful, to find a spot,
Where angels seem to trod.
A place akin to paradise
A place so close to God.

❦

The Favored Spice

I use exotic spices
To compliment each dish.
With distinct and zestful flavors
They become delish.

When it comes to daily living
To make things sweet and nice,
It's been tested, yes and proven.
Love is the favored spice.

Wallpaper Flowers

I can't afford the finer things.
Those dreams are miles away.
The only flowers to grace my home,
Are wallpaper bouquets.

I have tulips in the kitchen,
And roses in the hall.
Here in the sitting room,
Are hydrangeas wall to wall.

How glad I am to have them,
These gardens faded but quaint.
Forever blooming through the house
I'll have no need to paint.

My Grandpa

I remember his eyes, all misty
When he sang those gentle words.
I remember those sweet melodies,
More lovely than I'd ever heard.

And then, he'd tell me stories.
He'd brush away a tear.
Telling how it was when he was young,
Back there in yesteryear.

My grandpa was a special man.
His hands were big and strong,
But he could melt my heart,
When he broke into song.

How I miss that gentle man.
He gave meaning to my world.
He taught me the beauty of words,
When I was just a little girl.

Fairy Tale

A little girl on her Daddy's knee,
Was just a fairy tale, to me.
I'd wish, I'd wait, and I'd pretend,
But, I was never even his friend.

The years passed so quickly by,
So many times I wondered why.
And, all of those wishes that I had,
Were wished for you and me, Dad.

ᘓᕲᕗ

At Sunset

At sunset,
The pumpkin pie sun
Snuggles beneath
Whipped cream
Clouds.

Afternoon Tea

My copper kettle
Whistles merrily
And signals
That it's time for tea.
The fine china cups
Are filled with the brew.
There's lemon and sugar
And sweet cream too.
But, best of all there's friendship
Between you and me,
As we lovingly share
Our afternoon tea.

ꞔꙨꙩꞕ

Antique Shop

This musty, dusty menagerie
That's labeled Antique Shop,
Is filled with bits of yesteryear.
I can't resist the stop.

I rummage through the china,
The books and the chairs.
Then I spot a sign that reads,
There's more downstairs.

Quaint dolls with china faces.
Old lace and thread on reels.
Rocking baby carriages
And fine old spinning wheels.

Rummaging is half the fun,
Each book and dish, a pleasure.
But you can bet I'll come away,
With just the finest treasure.

My Patchwork Quilt

My patchwork quilt
Was stitched with care.
Mama sewed love
Into every square.

From leftover pieces
Of gingham and lace,
She worked many hours
Sewing patches in place.

I'd snuggle beneath it,
Away from all harm.
When the snow piled high,
I was cozy and warm.

Today it's displayed,
So that all might see.
The quilt Mama stitched,
Especially for me.

❦

My Christmas Wish

You need not bring me fancy gifts
To set upon the shelves.
I only wish that you will come,
Just bring yourselves.

Christmas should be a happy time,
To build our memories.
I only hope that you will come,
To share that time with me.

The lights will shine much brighter.
The holly, will sweeter be.
Won't you open up your hearts?
Give of yourselves, generously.

Summer Delights

Summer sounds
Are sheer delight,
The songs of wind chimes
In the night.

The fluted call
Of the whippoorwill,
The chatter of crickets
When night is still.

The distant whistle
Of an old freight train.
The pitter-patter
Of the falling rain.

The whispered rustle
Of lush green leaves,
Kissed by summer's
Sensual breeze.

‿◎◞

Summer's Golden Arms

Summer's golden arms embrace
A sky of azure-blue.
She paints the flowers, row on row
With bold and pastel hue.

She summons fresh sweet rain
To nourish all the land,
Then warms the earth with sunshine
That makes it all so grand.

My Son

How I miss those sparkling bright eyes,
The elfin grin he wore.
His little tattered tennis shoes,
The hand prints 'round the door.

His little faded blue jeans
With holes in both the knees.
And, I'm sure he got them
While climbing apple trees.

The baseball cards he scattered.
His crumpled, unkempt bed.
The visored hat he always wore
Sideways on his head.

Yes, I miss that little boy.
And, the things that remind me of him.
Thank goodness he hasn't lost
That sweet impish, elfin grin!!

ᥫᦡᦸᥫᦸ

Friendly Advice

Love is soft and fragile
Like the petals of the rose.
It needs nurturing care,
To make sure it grows.

But, like the rose,
The thorns are there.
This advice I give to you,
Approach each one with care!

My Paper Doll World

I'd like to go back to that carefree play,
Of a barefoot boy and a curly-top girl.
I'd like to go back to those childhood days,
Back to my paper doll world.

I'd like to turn back the hands of time,
Step back into yesterdays.
When all those hopes and dreams were mine,
Back in those paper doll days.

In Grand Array

When autumn's sun
Warms my face,
I close my mind
To time and space.

And hear the rustling
Rippling sound,
Of her leaves dancing
All around.

The gold, the crimson,
A burnished display,
Falls at my feet
In grand array.

എൊ൭ൟ

Lovely Burnished Autumn

Autumn is a lovely time.
A golden-crimson harvest time.
Summer's taken her farewell bow
And spring has been before the plow.
Now lovely-burnished autumn is sublime.

છુઠેળ

I Forgive

You wrinkle up your pretty nose
And scowl at my advice.
Again, you do your own thing,
Never pausing to think twice.

You leave me here with broken pieces,
Of mistakes I cannot fix.
Then, you stuff your haughty attitude
Into your bag of tricks.

You always whimper back to me
Demanding more than I can give.
Then, you wrinkle up your pretty nose
And once again, I forgive.

Morning Glory Mornings

Morning Glories at my window
Trailing roses on the fence
Violets in the rockery
Alyssum sweet and dense.

Coffee right for sipping
A blue bird on the wing.
Summer mornings in my garden
Are quite a lovely thing.

A comfy bench for dreaming.
A wall for privacy.
Here beneath my arbor
I find serenity.

∽⊙⊙∾

The Fickle River

The fickle river makes its bed,
Beside the aspen and the pine.
Then, it rushes off to meet
The honeysuckle vine.

It scatters driftwood pillows
In careless disarray.
Then, with each golden sunbeam,
It dances through the day.

Each time the moon is full,
And casts its silvery light,
The river dons its diamonds,
And dances through the night.

Loneliness

Beyond the wind
A whisper
I speak your name
And loneliness
Comes rushing
Back again.
With every song,
A memory.
My heart cries out to you
And teardrops
Rushing, crushing,
Keep me ever blue.
Without a dream
There's nothing.
Old heartaches return
To taunt and torture
My soul and tears
Forever burn.

∾

Heaven's Gift

She's but a blossom of a girl,
A flower growing wild.
A mischievous, adventurous,
Sun-bronzed child.

She's honey-sweet, full of charm.
And, glowing with sunshine.
She is truly heaven's gift
This child of mine.

First Snowfall

Winds whistle through the night.
I watch hearth embers glowing bright.

Inside, my world is cozy warm,
With anticipation I await the dawn.

I know I'll find a wonderland.
The first glance will be so grand.

Crystal prism's will grace the trees.
While snowflakes glisten brilliantly.

And banked against the picket fence,
I'll find diamonds, cool and dense.

⁓◦◉◦⁓

New Snow

I awoke to find my lawn encased
In jewels and sparkling bright.
Mother Nature's fashion show,
Traveled throughout the night.

Then, the huge spotlight sun,
Highlighted her grand design.
Accentuating, all the finest gems,
Mother Nature had left behind.

Discovery

I've found a quiet
Country road,
Where fields are filled
With black and gold.

Where Black-eyed Susan's
Tall and dense
Spill on through
A split-rail fence.

Where Queen Anne's lace
Grows wild and free,
Like fancy French-knot
Filigree.

It warms my heart
To find this place
So filled with gentle
Country grace.

⊷◉◌৲

Down Here on Memory Lane

Lonesomeness gets awful loud
Down here on memory lane.
Some day's I can't recollect
Why I've come here once again.

Wasn't there a brown-eyed boy
Waiting for me at the bend?
And, a little girl with golden curl?
But, I can't remember when.

Each time I pass the looking glass
A stranger stares back at me
And asks me for directions
To the lane of memory.

It's evident that over time
Shadowy images are eager to replace
All the loved ones there
Distorting every loving face.

My golden years are clouded,
Is senility to blame?
For all I see are strangers
Strolling, now, on memory lane.

Lonesomeness rings in my ears
Like the bell of requiem.
Will I ever again see clearly enough
To stroll down memory lane?

What Artist Could Resist

What artist could resist
The changing countryside?
Red's and gold's fairly drip
With newly painted pride.

No mortal's brush could paint
A scene so glorious.
Only GOD could master this,
To show His love for us.

~⊙~

The Last Star Is Mine

I remember when you told me
That star up there was mine.
The last one in the dipper,
My, how it did shine!

And now, each time I see it,
I can't help but smile.
At that heavenly little diamond
You gave me with such style.

Tea Party

Little girls with tiny tea cups
Pouring imaginary tea.
They're serving make believe scones
And chattering with glee.

Each wearing frilly oversized hats
And strands of opera length pearls.
Steeped in a world of lets pretend,
My precious rosy cheeked girls.

ᴄᴏᴏᴏ

Child Of Love

She's soft and pink and velvet-like,
This new born child of love.
And placed into my arms with care,
A gift, from GOD above.

I look into her searching eyes
With joy and wonderment.
I pray that I'll be worthy of
This child that GOD has sent.

Raindrops

Winter's bondage holds them fast
With icy-frigid shrouds.
Until, at last, those first raindrops
Are released from puffy clouds.

Then, like magic, petals dance
On tender new green stems
And all of nature revels in
Spring's beauty once again.

⌒⊙⌒

Words

Look at all the words
I can get
From twenty-six letters.
The alphabet,
If I scramble them up
And arrange them to rhyme
I come up with a verse
Every time.

I can write letters
That tell of my plans.
Assemble them for thank-you's
For wishes and commands.
Only twenty-six letters
It astonishes me
They spell every word
From A to Z.

Wet Paint

Let me dabble
To my hearts content
My paintings
Will never pay the rent.
I'll set up my easel
When I get the urge
And, be amazed
With whatever might emerge.

What care I
If I smudge my face
And, splatter paints
All over the place.
The surmounting messes
I'll deal with these
Who knows,
I might turn out a masterpiece!!!

എൟു

A Game You Play

Make a promise, break a promise,
And with it break a heart.
Take a dream, shape a dream,
Then, tear that dream apart.

It's all part of a game you play.
You stack the deck to win.
Make a promise, break a promise,
Then break a heart again.

❧᧞

In Memory's Garden

I've been harvesting today
In memory's garden fair.
I picked for you, the brightest dreams
That I found thriving there.
Along with dreams, I gathered cares
Growing tenderly.
I bring this dear bouquet to you
To keep you close to me.

⊲⊙⊚⊳

June Beauties

I'm captured by the charm
Of old-fashioned hollyhocks,
And sunny afternoons
That boast of four-o-clocks.

I'm so thrilled to see
There along the terraced wall,
Multi-colored phlox
Standing proud and tall.

Oh, what a joy it is for me
Each sun-kissed afternoon.
To view these graceful beauties
At their best in June.

If It Weren't For Bad Luck

If financial stability is a must,
I tell you kid, I'm nearly bust.
Poverty and yours truly
Are walking the line.
Take it from me
I can't rustle up a dime.
My horses aren't running
My numbers are all wrong.
I've exhausted my options,
They were not very strong.
Lottery players
Are winning each day.
While my chances
Are slipping away.
I tell you, friend,
It's as baffling as can be,
Why is it Lady Luck,
Never smiles on me???

୧୭ଚ

My Reflection

I know a secret, I tell her,
As I peer into the looking glass.
But, I'm not fooling her at all,
She knows my present and my past.

Her face has grown much older,
I see a sadness born of time.
When her eyes are tearful,
Then, so are mine.

I can never ever fool her.
She knows my secret heart.
And, it's always been that way
From the very start.

This reflection in the mirror
Is aging gracefully.
Sometimes, I think I catch a glimpse
Of the little girl I used to see.

My Fill

I don't think
I'll ever get my fill
Of early morning symphonies,
The song of the whip-poor-will.

Or dew on arbor roses.
Or daisies blowing free.
The air spiced with jasmine
Is just heavenly.

Or evenings as the sun
Nestles behind the hill.
No, I don't think
I'll ever get my fill.

ഛൈൟ

The Lovely Maple

In springtime the lovely maple
Wears her emerald gown.
In autumn she wears crimson
And lets it tumble down.

She stands tall in summer's beauty
With pride and gracefulness.
She's lovely through all seasons
But in autumn she's at her best.

My Garden Of Memories

When I'm lonely, I can go
To a special place I know.
An enchanted garden of memory
That thrives so vividly.

Blossoms of remembrances stand tall.
I harvest them, one and all.
And keep the seeds to sow anew,
Petals of love, which I grow, for you.

༺◎◎༻

Indifference

It was not so much his attitude
Or the fact he'd told me those lies,
But, rather that cold defiance
In his tattle-tale eyes.

It was not so much his wandering ways
Or the fact he'd boasted of such,
But, rather the cold indifference
In his touch.

Seasons Of The Heart

Summer's gone
When gold leaves fall.
Do you hear
Winter's call?
Our seasons come
And quickly go.
The summer winds
No longer blow.
When spring returns
Fresh and new
My heart, again
Yearns for you.

༼ᖴᘖᖳ༽

Christmas Eve

How bright the lights of Christmas,
Glow in windows everywhere.
How lovely, soft, fresh, snowflakes float
Upon the frosty air.

How sweetly holly berries grace
The fresh cut evergreen.
How dear the midnight silence is,
On this Christmas Eve.

The Image In The Mirror

The mirror is not kind to me.
It does not hide the pain.
The years are here upon my face,
Reminding me again.

My childhood seems a blur to me.
And too, my teen age years.
My young adulthood found me busy,
Drying others' tears.

Now, here I am at middle age,
With someone else's face.
Watching days and years roll by,
At a frightening pace.

The young ones call me Grandma,
And time keeps rushing by.
The image in the mirror,
Is one I can't deny.

ﻌﻮﻮ

Finis

How well I remember
That autumn day.
When the swirling winds
Seemed to whisk away,
The love we shared
All the dreams we had,
We watched them go
Oh, how sad.

You didn't look back
To see my tears fall.
Your ears were deafened
To my heart's call.
But strangely enough
I felt at ease.
A sad serene calm,
A welcoming peace.

I Can't Think Of A Nicer Spot

I can't think of a nicer spot
To spend the morning hours.
Than right here in my garden,
Amid the fragrant flowers.

The warm sun kissing my face
While birds sing sweet melodies.
I can't think of a nicer place
In all of the world to be.

In the twilight hour,
At the close of each day,
Right here, in my garden,
Is where I'll stay.

☙◉❧

September Day

We set out in search of color
On a bright September day.
We found them crisp and glorious.
All along the way.
The red's and gold's, the russets
Blended with shades of green.
Were the most memorable
I think I've ever seen.

Renewal

The old tree looks sad and barren,
Its branches dry and brown.
Unprotected against the wind,
It's bent and drooping down.

Red birds stop awhile to rest
And, with a blue jay's trill,
The tree becomes quite elegant,
And soon its branches fill.

I hear the merry songs they sing,
These bright feathered friends,
And for just a little while
The tree comes to life again.

എൈഌ

Wishful Thinking

My diet's made me delirious,
I knew someday it would.
Everyone keeps telling me,
It's for my own good.

The clouds I see up in the sky,
Are not clouds at all.
They're meringue topped lemon pies,
I wish that one would fall.

ENCORE PLEASE

She started off
With Turkey-in-the-straw,
Then, on to Humoresque.
These were a couple of the many tunes
She played upon request.
She drew her bow
Across the strings
And played until night fall.
We always told her
She and her violin
Belonged at Carnegie Hall.
We imagined
The curtain going up
And we pleaded for more.
She drew her bow
Across the strings
And played an encore.
Then, into our dreams
Those songs would steal
With a concert about to begin.
As we drifted off
To the melodies
From, Mom's old violin.

⁓൧ၜ൧⁓

If I Could Go Back

If I could go back,
Return to days of old,
I'd be more careful
Whose hands I'd hold.

I'd tread more cautiously
And learn to recognize
A smooth-talker
With tattle-tale eyes.

I'd be more mindful,
I'd take special care
Not to leave my heart
Just anywhere.

Pastels

Pastel colors
Of the morning,
Subdued, muted
Like Monet paintings.
Reflecting in dewdrops.
Serene, calming
Unobtrusive tones
Soothing mind
And soul.
Pastels.

༄༅

Little Boy

I've mopped up his muddy footprints.
Scrubbed crayon off the walls.
I've picked up the toys he scattered
Up and down the halls.

I've cleaned and bandaged bruises.
I've wiped his tears away.
I know the footprints he left upon my heart
Are all here to stay.

⌒∾⊚∾⌒

Back In Memory

The whispering wind
Speaks your name
And takes me back
To your arms again.

Your face is reflected
In each smile I see
And once again I'm back
Back in memory.

❧

The Beauty Of Summer

I do so love the songbirds,
The scarlet maple trees.
Summer's painted daisies
And the busy honey bees.
Yes, I admire the hollyhocks
The faded stockade fence.
The arbor and the dahlias
The ivy trailing dense.
The climbing rose enchants me
Glistening with dew.
Fluffy cotton candy clouds
Enhance a sky of blue.
It seems my good fortune
The beauties summer brings.
And, I enjoy them all
From my garden swing.

Where Lilies Bloom

In fields along the roadways
Throughout this great land,
It's there I see the touch
Of the Master's loving hand.

I find lilies flourishing
With love and gentle care.
Their loveliness inspires in me
A silent, reverent prayer.

❦

These Wonders

It's a puzzlement,
A wonder to me,
How an acorn becomes
A giant oak tree,

And this unsightly twig
All twisted and bent,
Can bring forth blossoms
With their marvelous scent.

The immortal artist
Smiles down from above,
And gives us these wonders
With undying love.

Autumn's Garden

Autumn's garden holds a promise
That spring will not be long.
Birds serenade me from the willow
With their farewell song.

The wind is whispering adios
Along the winding path.
And bluebirds stop to bid adieu
In a ring around my old bird bath.

୧ବ୍ଓ

She's A Dear Sweet Lady

She's a dear sweet lady
With her encouraging style.
She brightens the sunlight
With her magical smile.

She holds close in her heart,
Great dreams for my world.
She tells me each day,
I'm her special girl.

She dries all my teardrops.
She kisses away the pain,
Smiles and soothes my hurts,
Time and time again.

Oh, how I love her.
She is Mother to me.
She's embroidering my heart
With sweet memories.

White Roses

My lovely, antique, crystal vase,
Has held many fragrant bouquets.
But, none so elegant, my love,
As the roses it now displays.

What a precious gift you brought to me,
Like pure snowdrops clustered there.
I've always loved the yellow rose
But, these are just as fair.

Valentine gifts, have always been,
Chocolates and lacey things.
I can't begin to tell you dear,
Of the joy your bouquet brings.

ॐ

I Never Knew

I never knew grandmother love.
Never felt that soft embrace.
I never saw time-etched lines
Upon a gentle face.

I never heard the lullabies
She'd have sung to me.
Deep in my heart are the feelings
Of what would never be.

I never heard the gentle voice,
Never a soft hand touching mine.
Never the stories she could tell,
Only in my dreams I seek to find.

Still, I feel her here with me
It's her presence I truly miss.
Perhaps the breeze upon my cheek
Is really her sweet kiss.

My own grandchildren laugh with me.
And now, I hold them dear.
They hear the stories and the songs,
I always longed to hear.

City Dog

My poor little city dog
You can't run free,
You're chained instead.
Your world is very small
You sleep in a cradle,
A dolly's bed.
But, the saddest thing yet,
I observed you there
Burying another bone,
In my over-stuffed chair.

⋙⋘

My Mother's Teapot

Some teapots are plain
Others, elegant in form.
Some are ornate
And away from the norm.

Some brightly painted
With roses and such.
Others decorated
With a personal touch.

I have a favorite.
It's special to me.
Just plain white porcelain,
No eccentricity.

It has a small chip
At the edge of the spout.
But, it doesn't matter
When the tea flows out.

My Mother's teapot
Is priceless to me.
And each cup is sweetened
By her memory.

Home With You

I travel country roads and highways
With mountain tops in view,
Yet, in my heart each path I travel,
Leads me home to you.

Ocean waves and city maze
No matter where I roam,
There is no place I'd rather be
Than here, with you, at home.

cଡ଼ଡ଼

Farewell

Farewell to songbirds
Farewell to summertime.
Farewell to the roses
And the morning glory vine.

Farewell to the garden-spot
With its abundant yield.
Farewell to sweet daisies
Blowing in the field.

Farewell to sun-bronzed days
And the cool evening breeze.
Farewell to star-lit nights
And lacy green trees.

Farewell to youth
And to glorious springtime.
Farewell to the dreams
I thought were mine.

Sweet Pleasures

None is more pleasing
To a passer-by
Then billowy clouds
In a pale blue sky.
Or trailing roses
On an arbor swing
And golden sunshine
The mornings bring.

≈⊙≈

The First Day Of May

The first day of May
Should sunny be,
With lilac and tulip
And budding tree.

With sunshine and dewdrops
And bunnies and such,
Surely, not snowflakes
And, not this much!

The One's Here In My Heart

In the back of my minds eye,
Where my vision is very clear,
I keep a store of memories,
The lot is oh so dear.

Now and then they surface,
Fresh as at the start,
But, they cannot compare
To the one's here in my heart.

❧❀❧

Token

Rain falls softly
On flowers and hills.
It fills buttercups
And daffodils.
It splashes window panes.
And helps gardens grow.
Then, leaves us a token,
A splendid rainbow.

He Who Works a Garden Plot

I believe that from the time
The first seed is sown,
He who works a garden plot
Does not toil alone.

From the time each shoot emerges
Until the growing season's done,
We cannot give the credit
To just the rain and sun.

For the Almighty Creator
Blessed all the land.
He who works a garden plot,
Is guided by God's hand.

❧

Dancing Leaves

I thought I saw leaves dancing,
Across the pale blue sky.
Skimming, dipping, swirling,
But, they were butterflies.

What a lovely autumn day.
The pumpkin-sun so bright.
And I, in awe, am honored
By this lovely sight.

Fish Tales

The falling rain
Cannot detain
An eager fisherman.

He makes his way
Through foggy-haze,
With rod and reel in hand.

He casts all day
Under skies of gray
Waiting for a bite.

And then comes back
With fish all wrapped
In paper crisp and white.

Then, late at night,
By the warm fire light
He talks about his day.

With laughter he wails,
As he tells us the tales
Of the ones that got away.

❦

Country Girl

I am not kin
To Kings or Queens
Or any royalty.
There is no need
For me to trace
My genealogy.

For I was born
A country girl
Into simplicity,
With all the riches
This great land
Could bestow upon me.

❦

The Chinese Rose

The bush beneath my window stands,
In drifts of jeweled snow.
In springtime it becomes so grand,
The lovely Chinese rose.

It's dainty branches, laden then,
With blossoms bowing down,
Like a million ballerina's
In their lovely perfumed gowns.

❧❧❧

Whisper Softly

Whisper softly near the roses
So not a petal falls.
They are fragile, living wonders
I treasure them all.

Their life span is very short
But, oh so wonderful.
Whisper softly near the roses
Make it meaningful.

When winter winds blow cold
And the bushes look forlorn.
Whisper softly to the roses
Beware, the prickly thorn.

Remember, too, that summer time
Will bring forth buds anew.
Whisper softly near the roses,
They will comfort you.

꩜

Beware of Thorns

GOD made the roses to enjoy,
The thorns but to endure.
Proof of beauty's imperfections,
A lesson to be learned.

Pick the rose with greatest care,
Drink its sweet perfume.
Just remember to beware
Of thorns on every bloom.

ఇౠ౷

My Rose Bush

My charming little rose bush,
Slumbers deep beneath the snow.
A ruby-velvet masterpiece
Of beauty to behold.

The kiss of rain sweet and warm.
The sun's bright golden rays,
Will gently awaken sleepy buds
For summer's sweet bouquets.

cɔ๑ɕɔ

Stop Awhile

Stop awhile to smell the roses
For summer travels fast,
She's here all fresh in pastels
But her beauty will not last.

Today there is enchantment
Along the garden walk,
So, I will stop to smell the roses
And admire the hollyhock.

಄ಀಀ

So Long

Goodbye is such a cold word,
So final and so empty.
It means that in the stretch of a lifetime
We may never meet again.
It means erasing from one's heart
And mind, all the things we have been.
Goodbye is forever, the breaking of a bond,
It's the end of a way of life.
It's the saddest word in Webster's book.
A word that goes along with tears.
I prefer to say so long.

About the Author

⚜

Marianna Jo was born in Monticello, MN. The second child, in a family of eight children, she was just 3yrs. old when her parents moved the family to a farm near Hanover, MN. There was never a shortage of work, laughter, love, or excitement in their large family.

She is a graduate of Buffalo High School, Buffalo, MN.

As the mother of five children, and step-mother of two, she has been blessed with grandchildren and great-grandchildren.

Marianna Jo's interests and hobbies are as varied as her poetry and short stories. Among them are cooking, quilting, reading, painting, traveling, gardening, and of course her writing. Each member of her family proudly displays a treasured quilt, handmade especially for them, by Marianna Jo.

A tour of Europe in 1984, which Marianna Jo made with her Mother, was outstanding. They created many warm, and wonderful, life-long memories.

She has been a member of the Red Hat Society's Glad Hatter's for the past three years. This lively group meets to share their lives, laughter, libations, and much more, once a month over lunch.

Marianna Jo makes her home in Big Lake, MN. She and husband Carl both love to travel the United States by car or train.

They spend many pleasurable hours caring for their rose gardens and feeding the fine feathered friends that inhabit and enjoy their backyard flower gardens as much as their family, friends and neighbors do.

Printed in the United States
107996LV00001B/145/P